Quotable Hollywood

Quotable Hollywood

The Lowdown from America's Film Capital

George Sullivan

BARNES
&NOBLE
BOOKS
NEW YORK

2001 Barnes & Noble Books

Text design by Lundquist Design, New York

ISBN 0-7607-2387-7

Printed and bound in the United States of America

01 02 03 04 05 06 M 9 8 7 6 5 4 3 2 1
RRD-H

*For Eleanor Sullivan, a Hollywood enthusiast
who would have liked this book . . .*

*And Kevin "Chuck" Connors, the Rifleman,
who would have, too . . .*

*And producer Paul Keyes's
beloved Miriam, who makes three.*

Special Credits to . . .

Literary agent Cynthia Manson and editor Beth Tripmacher, who shone in Best Supporting roles . . .

And to my heroine, Betty, who stars every day.

Contents

Hooray for

Hollywood

Hooray for Hollywood

Hollywood's a place where they'll pay you a thousand dollars for a kiss and 50 cents for your soul.
— *Marilyn Monroe*

You can seduce a man's wife there, attack his daughter, and wipe your hands on his canary. But if you don't like his movie, you're dead.
— *Josef von Sternberg,* director

To survive there, you need the ambition of a Latin American revolutionary, the ego of a grand opera tenor, and the physical stamina of a cow pony.
— *Billie Burke*

All Hollywood corrupts, and absolute Hollywood corrupts absolutely.
— *Edmund Wilson*

———

Paradise with a lobotomy.
— *Anonymous*

———

A gilded slum.
— *Adela Rogers St. Johns*

———

Hollywood is a sewer—with service from the Ritz Carlton.
— *Wilson Mizner*

———

In this town a girl better be ready for anything—from something that sweeps her off her feet to something that knocks her on her ass.
— *Marisa Tomei*

———

Hollywood is like being nowhere and talking to nobody about nothing.
— *Michelangelo Antonioni,* Italian director

Hooray for Hollywood

A place where the inmates are in charge of the asylum.
— *Laurence Stallings,* screenwriter

———

There is nothing wrong with Hollywood that six first-class funerals wouldn't solve.
— *Anonymous*

———

Everyone in Hollywood is looking for the blockbuster. They tell you their last movie "only grossed $70 million," as if that were some kind of crime.
— *Neil Simon* in 1990

———

Two of the cruelest, most primitive punishments our town deals out to those who fall from favor are the empty mailbox and the silent telephone.
— *Hedda Hopper*

———

In Hollywood you can be forgotten while you're out of the room going to the toilet.
— *Anonymous*

Quotable Hollywood

It's somehow symbolic of Hollywood that Tara was just a facade, with no rooms inside.
> — *David O. Selznick,* who built it in the 1939 classic, *Gone with the Wind*

It's redundant to die in California.
> — *Truman Capote*

If you want to be a success in Hollywood, be sure and go to New York.
> — *Bert Lahr*

I came out here with one suit and everybody said I looked like a bum. Twenty years later Marlon Brando comes out with only a sweatshirt and the town drools over him. That shows you how much Hollywood has progressed.
> — *Humphrey Bogart*

A Hollywood triangle is made up of an actor, his wife, and himself.
> — *Henny Youngman*

Hooray for Hollywood

This is where I have wasted the best years of my life.
— *Greta Garbo*

I believe that God felt sorry for actors, so He created Hollywood to give them a place in the sun and a swimming pool. The price they had to pay was to surrender their talent.
— *Sir Cedric Hardwicke*

It's a scientific fact that if you stay in California, you lose one point of IQ for every year.
— *Truman Capote*

Hollywood is a place where your best friend will plunge a knife in your back and then call the police to tell them that you are carrying a concealed weapon.
— *George Frazier,* columnist and critic

A kingdom like Oz.
— *Adela Rogers St. Johns*

I don't do the Hollywood party scene any more. You can't come home and say to the kid, "Hi, here's a little switch. Daddy's going to throw up on you."
— *Robin Williams*

I don't think Hollywood made me turn to drugs. It just made it easier for me to get them.
— *Drew Barrymore,* recalling earlier days

The same damn people, saying the same damn things. All that changes is the women's dresses.
— *John Wayne,* explaining why he ducked most Hollywood parties

When it's 100 in New York, it's 72 in Los Angeles. When it's 30 in New York, it's 72 in Los Angeles. However, there are six-million interesting people in New York—and 72 in Los Angeles.
— *Neil Simon*

All the sincerity in Hollywood you can stuff in a flea's navel and still have room to conceal eight caraway seeds and an agent's heart.
— *Fred Allen*

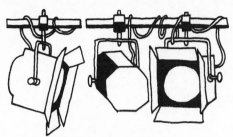

Lights!

Camera!

Action!

Lights! Camera! Action!

━━◆━━

The Academy of Motion Picture Arts and Sciences? What art? What science?
— *D. W. Griffith,* early moviemaker

━─━

I feel very strongly that the director is supposed to be the boss. Art was never created by democracy.
— *Charlton Heston*

━─━

No one ever went broke in Hollywood underestimating the intelligence of the public.
— *Elsa Maxwell,* professional party giver

━─━

I read part of it all the way through.
— *Samuel Goldwyn*

Quotable Hollywood

In the inexplicable film world, cowardice increases in relation to the amount of money invested.
— *Peter Ustinov*

———

Today, you see girls doing on the screen what they used to do *off* the screen to get *on* the screen.
— *Gene Autry*

———

In my day we made films that had class. Today, if class sneaks into a picture, it's by accident. I'm of the old school and proud of it.

I find suggestion a hell of a lot more provocative than explicit detail. You didn't see Clark [Gable] and Vivien [Leigh] rolling around in bed in *Gone with the Wind,* but you saw that shit-eating grin on her face the next morning and you knew damned well she'd gotten properly laid.

The impact was stronger because of the subtlety.
— *Joan Crawford*

———

The happy ending in many films is the fact the picture has ended.
— *Henny Youngman*

Lights! Camera! Action!

In the theater, you actually have writers. Here [in Hollywood], if somebody writes *The Karate Kid,* they think they've got fucking Faulkner on their hands.
— *James Woods*

If writers ever realize how important they are, they'll take it all over.
— Attributed to Columbia's *Harry Cohn* and other studio heads

---

I'd hire the devil himself as a writer if he gave me a good story.
— *Samuel Goldwyn*

I always thought the actors were hired to ruin the writer's lines.
— *Robert Benton,* screenwriter and director

Acting engenders and harbors qualities that are best left way behind in adolescence. People-pleasing, going on those interviews and jamming your whole personality into getting the job, ingratiating yourself to people you wouldn't fucking spit on if they were on fire.
— *Carrie Fisher* in a 1990 interview with *Vanity Fair*

A masochistic form of exhibitionism. It is not quite the occupation of an adult.
   — *Laurence Olivier* on acting, which he described as "just one big bag of tricks"

———

Show biz is a great haven for weirdos like me.
   — *Roseanne*

———

Acting, not prostitution, is the oldest profession. Even apes act.
   — *Marlon Brando*

———

Acting is the most minor of gifts and not a very high-class way to earn a living . . .
   Never forget that they don't give a Nobel Prize for it, and that Shirley Temple was doing it perfectly adequately at the age of 4.
   — *Katharine Hepburn*

———

Why do actors think they're so goddamn important? They're not. Acting is not an *important* job in the scheme of things. Plumbing is.
   — *Spencer Tracy*

Lights! Camera! Action!

Disney, of course, has the best casting. If he doesn't like an actor, he just tears him up.
— *Alfred Hitchcock*

———

Some of my best leading men have been dogs and horses.
— *Elizabeth Taylor*

———

It's holding up books on the bookcase downstairs—and the gold is flaking.
— *Jane Fonda* on the whereabouts of one of her two Best Actress Oscars—one for 1971's *Klute,* the other for 1978's *Coming Home*

———

I don't know . . . [pause, mulling the question] . . . I think my secretary has it.
— *Marlon Brando,* when Larry King asked where his Oscar was

———

I adore not being me. I'm not very good at being me. That's why I adore acting so much.
— *Deborah Kerr*

Quotable Hollywood

Throughout my career I was paid for doing what 9-year-old kids get punished for.
— *Jerry Lewis*

If I play a stupid girl and ask a stupid question, I've got to follow it through. What am I supposed to do—look intelligent?
— *Marilyn Monroe*

The only way to succeed is to make people hate you. That way they remember you.
— *Josef von Sternberg*

They shoot too many pictures and not enough actors.
— *Walter Winchell*, columnist

An actor's a guy who, if you ain't talking about him, ain't listening.
— *Marlon Brando*

Acting is cheap group therapy, being a schizo 50 different ways. And we're paid!
— *Sally Struthers*

Lights! Camera! Action!

For an actress to be a success she must have the face of Venus, the brains of Minerva, the grace of Terpsichore, the memory of Macaulay, the figure of Juno, and the hide of a rhinoceros.
— *Ethel Barrymore*

You're only as good as your last picture.
— *Marie Dressler,* probably the first to say what became a Hollywood adage

---

Never take top billing. You'll last longer that way.
— *Bing Crosby*

Take the big part, but hold off [on buying] the big house and the Cadillac or you'll be in hock to the studios for the rest of your life.
— *Humphrey Bogart*'s advice to two young actors

All they ever did for me at MGM was change my leading men and the water in my pool.
— *Esther Williams*

If I'd been screwed by my husbands as I was by Warner's, I'd still be married.
— *Cher,* who once directed anger at another studio by imprinting her Metro tee-shirt with rhinestones spelling *MGM SUCKS*

It's better than being a pimp.
— *Harry Cohn* on the business of making movies

Don't worry. We'll run next door to RKO. They haven't had a hit in years.
— *Bing Crosby* to fellow workers on a Paramount set early in World War II, when alarm was expressed that the studio could be a target of enemy bombers because it resembled a factory from the air

We're selling corn, and I like corn.
— *Walt Disney*

I used to wonder if there wasn't a sub-human species of woman-kind that bred children for the sole purpose of dragging them to Hollywood.
— *Hedda Hopper*

Lights! Camera! Action!

Anyone who hits the top as a child star has no place to go but down.
  — *Linda Blair,* recalling making 1973's *The Exorcist* as "hell"—before growing up into "B" pictures

---

Method acting? There are quite a few methods. Mine involves a lot of talent, a glass, and some cracked ice.
  — *John Barrymore*

My dear boy, you look absolutely awful. Why don't you try *acting*? It's so much easier.
  — *Laurence Olivier* to Dustin Hoffman when the latter reportedly arrived on 1976's *Marathon Man* set worn out by his "method" preparations

---

Awards are nice, but I'd much rather have a job.
  — *Jane Darwell,* accepting her 1940 Supporting Actress Oscar for *The Grapes of Wrath*

Quotable Hollywood

I hope to God I don't win an Oscar. It would really depress me if I did.
> — *Dustin Hoffman,* who won a couple for Best Actor anyway—for *Kramer vs. Kramer* in 1979 and for *Rain Man* in 1988

I tried to play a villain once, in 1935, in *After the Thin Man.* It's the only time I ever played a murderer, and the audience laughed me off the screen. I've been playing Jimmy Stewart ever since.
> — *James Stewart*

I have always hated that damn James Bond. I'd like to kill him.
> — *Sean Connery*

The embarrassing thing is that the salad dressing is out-grossing my films.
> — *Paul Newman,* actor and entrepreneur

Now I can do to actors what directors did to me.
> — *Anthony Perkins,* when he agreed to direct 1986's *Psycho III*
>
> *"Ha, ha—just kidding," Perkins added.*

Lights! Camera! Action!

Our relationship with agents can be summed up in a sentence: We pray they don't kill us in our sleep.

> — *Howard Rodman,* screenwriter

A strictly spontaneous ovation.

> — *Jesse Lasky*'s order for Paramount employees to gather en masse in front of the studio to welcome Gloria Swanson back from Europe

---

Beginner's luck.

> — *John Wayne* to presenter Barbra Streisand as he accepted the Best Actor Oscar for 1969's *True Grit,* Oscar and Duke finally getting together five decades after both giants came to Hollywood in 1928

For what—wrinkled sheets, burlap sacks, and loincloths?

> — *Rex Reed,* when *Gandhi* received 1982's Costume Design Oscar

---

I don't generally look at scripts . . . I don't care what [a film] is about. At $200,000 a week, what do I care what it's about?

> — *Mickey Rooney,* after six decades of making movies

Quotable Hollywood

Actors don't retire, they just get offered fewer roles.
— *David Niven*

———

When I drove through the studio gate and the thrill was gone, I knew it was time to quit.
— *James Cagney*

That's a

PROD. NO.

SCENE	TAKE	SOUND

DIRECTOR

CAMERAMAN

DATE

Wrap

That's a Wrap

Creation is a drug I can't do without.
— *Cecil B. DeMille*

If you want art, don't mess around with movies. Buy a Picasso.
— *Michael Winner,* director

I've always had a nightmare: I dream that one of my pictures has ended up in an art theater, and I wake up shaking.
— *Walt Disney*

It's only a movie, for God's sake!
— *Alfred Hitchcock,* responding to Kim Novak's reported "What is my character feeling in relation to her surroundings?" during filming of 1958's *Vertigo*

This is a terrific script. It just needs a complete rewrite.
— *Peter Bogdanovich* to Alvin Sargent while directing 1973's
Paper Moon

———

Let's bring it up to date with some snappy 19th-century
dialogue.
— *Samuel Goldwyn*

———

Give me a couple of pages of the Bible and I'll give you a
picture.
— *Cecil B. DeMille*

———

I loved it—particularly the ideas he took from me.
— *D. W. Griffith,* the film pioneer, after viewing Orson
Welles's 1941 classic, *Citizen Kane*

———

If I have to get up and piss, you'll know it's no good.
— *Jack Warner* to star/producer Warren Beatty and director
Arthur Penn as they arrived to show 1967's *Bonnie and
Clyde* to the mogul

That's a Wrap

The length of a film should be directly related to the endurance of the human bladder.
— *Alfred Hitchcock*

———

When I started making films, I wanted to make Frank Capra pictures. But I've never been able to make anything but these crazy, tough pictures. You are what you are.
— *John Cassavetes*

———

The bosom is not right. We're going to have to put something in there.
— *Alfred Hitchcock,* summoning costumer Edith Head to improve Grace Kelly's bustline during filming of 1954's *Rear Window,* when the actress appeared in a sheer negligée

———

What do you want me to do, stop shooting and release it as *The Five Commandments*?
— *Cecil B. DeMille* to Adolph Zukor when the studio boss fretted about the length of his 1923 version of *The Ten Commandments*

Quotable Hollywood

I didn't want the headaches, I didn't want *Marlon of Brando*.
— *Sam Spiegel,* producer, on why he opposed casting
Brando as 1962's *Lawrence of Arabia* as favored by director
David Lean

—•—

I derive no pleasure from the process of directing.
— *Francis Ford Coppola*

—•—

Relax!
— *Otto Preminger,* yelling it after creeping up behind a nervous actor on a tense set

—•—

I make my films with 18 good friends.
— *Ingmar Bergman,* while discussing crews with David Lean

I make mine with 150 enemies.
— *David Lean,* responding to Ingmar Bergman

—•—

To me, it's a fun picture.
— *Alfred Hitchcock* on *Psycho,* his 1960 classic superchiller

That's a Wrap

A director must be a policeman, a midwife, a psychoanalyst, a sycophant, and a bastard.
— *Billy Wilder*

Cry, you little monsters!
— *Otto Preminger,* urging a group of children to tears during filming of 1960's *Exodus*

Fine—that'll add some realism to the scene.
— *Irving Thalberg,* during filming of 1925's *Ben Hur,* when he ordered that there would be no lunch break for 4,300 extras and was told by production manager Joe Cohn, "But those people are hungry. They may riot."

Well, do something about it!
— *Barbra Streisand,* director/co-star, reportedly frustrated when the sun came up over Manhattan, spoiling lighting of a final scene in 1996's *The Mirror Has Two Faces*

Too caustic? To hell with the cost, we'll make the picture anyway.
— *Samuel Goldwyn*

With a play, I have only two people to please—myself and the director. With this movie, it was 19 executives, a director who'd never done anything but animation before, and two stars who would tell you what lines they'd say and what lines they wouldn't say.

— *Neil Simon* on making 1991's *The Marrying Man*

You are here to please me. Nothing else on earth matters.

— *Cecil B. DeMille* to his staff

An associate producer is the only guy in Hollywood who will associate with a producer.

— *Fred Allen*

Sweet Smell

# of Success

Sweet Smell of Success

It's like waking up with a hooker—*how the hell did I get here?*
— *Clint Eastwood* on achieving stardom

If you want a place in the sun, you have to expect a few blisters.
— *Loretta Young* on the price of stardom

There is no question you get pumped up by the recognition.
Then a self-loathing sets in when you realize you're enjoying it.
— *George C. Scott*

One thing about being successful is that I stopped being afraid
of dying. Once you're a star you're dead already. You're
embalmed.
— *Dustin Hoffman*

Remember you are a star. Never go across the alley even to dump garbage unless you are dressed to the teeth.
  — *Cecil B. DeMille* to Paulette Goddard

———

It's a strenuous job every day of your life to live up to the way you look on the screen.
  — *Jean Arthur*

———

Being a star has made it possible for me to get insulted in places where the average Negro could never hope to get insulted.
  — *Sammy Davis Jr.*

———

A fan club is a group of people who tell an actor he is not alone in the way he feels about himself.
  — *Jack Carson*

———

She's got talent and personality. Give me two years and I'll make her an overnight star.
  — *Harry Cohn* on young Kim Novak

Sweet Smell of Success

It's all happening too fast. I've got to put the brakes on or I'll smack into something.
— *Mel Gibson*

When *Back to the Future* first made it big, I kept a picture of John Belushi on my living-room wall. That was to remind me what could happen if I lost my head and my values over this fame thing.
— *Michael J. Fox*

Being a star doesn't really change you. If you become a star, *you* don't change—everybody else does.
— *Kirk Douglas* on how others treat and look at stars

A celebrity is a person who works hard all his life to become well known, then wears dark glasses to avoid being recognized.
— *Fred Allen*

I stopped believing in Santa Claus when I was 6. Mother took me to see him in a department store and he asked me for my autograph.
— *Shirley Temple*

Quotable Hollywood

Go away, go away! I don't need you any more!
— *Norma Talmadge,* shooing away autograph seekers as she
    exited a Hollywood restaurant after retiring

———

A friend recently said, "Just imagine *not* being famous—what
would happen?" And all of a sudden I saw the face of a passerby
on the street and the oddest feeling came over me.
— *Gloria Swanson*

———

Even when you win the rat race, you're still a rat.
— *Joan Collins*

What's in a Name?

What's in a Name?

———◆———

I don't remember anybody's name. Why do you think the "dahling" thing started?
   — *Eva Gabor*

———

Helen Hayes isn't a very fancy name, but I notice people have no trouble remembering it.
   — *George Abbott,* Broadway producer/director, warning
      young Gene Tierney not to let Hollywood tinker with her
      name—including the male name Gene

———

Wouldn't I have made up something a little more exciting?
   — *Betty White*'s response when asked if that was her
      real name

I'm glad I had a middle name to run to.
— *Eldred Gregory Peck*

The name's got to go . . . the critics will use it like a baseball bat. They'll kill you. They'll say Lemmon is a lemon. The picture is a lemon, everything connected with Lemmon is a lemon.

There's no way you can keep your name. You've got to change it.
— *Harry Cohn* to young Jack Lemmon while trying to convince him to change his name to Lennon

---

Get ridda that. Don't you change your name. Your father finds out, he's gonna kick your ass!
— *Dolly Sinatra* to son Francis, who was singing for tips under the name "Frankie Trent" at a New Jersey roadhouse in 1938

It sounds too much like "LeSewer."
— *Pete Smith,* MGM's publicity chief, urging boss Louis B. Mayer to change newcomer Lucille LeSueur's name . . . soon to become Joan Crawford
The young actress loathed her new name, protesting, "Joan Crawford*! It sounds like* Crawfish*!"*

What's in a Name?

I won't even have to change the initials on my towels.
— *Greta Gustafsson*, a budding Stockholm actress just turned 18, happily accepting a name change in 1923—the birth of Greta Garbo, easily pronounced in any language

———

I experienced hope that Victor Mature might eventually live up to his name, but I'm beginning to despair.
— *Hedda Hopper*

———

Oomph is the sound that a fat man makes when he leans over to tie his shoelaces in a telephone booth.
— *Ann Sheridan*, dismissing the "Oomph Girl" label pinned on her by a Warner's publicist

———

Richard and Elizabeth? I don't know any Elizabeth and Richard. Why don't people sign their last names?
— *Gig Young*, puzzled by a flower basket from Mr. & Mrs. Burton when he won a Best Supporting Oscar for 1969's *They Shoot Horses, Don't They?*

———

. . . Hedda Hopper and . . . and . . . what's the fat one?
— *Marlon Brando* trying to recall Louella Parsons's name on *Larry King Live* in 1994

Quotable Hollywood

Dear Sir: I do wish you would do something about the way my name is spelled in your newspaper from day to day. My name is Ivor Novello, not Ivan or Eva. For the life of me I cannot understand how people can get names wrong as does your Lulu Pearson!

— *Ivor Novello*'s letter to the editor of the Los Angeles newspaper that carried Louella Parsons's column

———

If we'd known it was the "Golden Age," we might have enjoyed it more.

— *Ann Rutherford* at a 1989 assembly of Hollywood veterans

Mirror, Mirror

Mirror, Mirror

———◆———

Mean. Spiteful. Short-tempered. Suspicious. Jealous. Selfish. Ungiving. Et cetera.
— *Walter Matthau* describing himself for Rex Reed

———

I was born at the age of 12 on a Metro-Goldwyn-Mayer lot.
— *Judy Garland*

———

I'm an actress, not a fad. I don't stand out in a crowd.
— *Diane Keaton,* explaining why she's happily not "hampered" by a big public profile

———

They don't see me as an actress, they see me as an icon, and it makes me extremely exhausted.
— *Madonna* on the technicians on her set

Quotable Hollywood

Sometimes I think that my life is a B-movie script. . . . I'd never make the movie.
— *Kirk Douglas*

I was Tiffany's, but they kept insisting on putting me in Woolworth's window.
— *Robert Alda* on what "ruined my career" at Warner Brothers in the Forties and Fifties

Everybody wants to be Cary Grant. Even *I* want to be Cary Grant.
— *Cary Grant*

I ain't really Hank Fonda. Nobody could be. Nobody could have that much integrity.
— *Henry Fonda* on his screen image

I'm so damned sick of Katharine Hepburn, I'd like to kill her. On second thought, people have been so nice to me lately because they think I'm going to die. Think I'll stick around awhile and make the most of it.
— *Katharine Hepburn*

Mirror, Mirror

I can't play myself! If you give me a gun, a cigarette, a wig, I can play any old bag, but I can't play myself!
  — *Bette Davis,* after repeatedly blowing her lines while playing herself in 1944's *Hollywood Canteen*—as recalled by co-star Joan Leslie

———

I never go out unless I look like Joan Crawford the movie star. If you want to see the girl next door, go next door.
  — *Joan Crawford*

———

I'm nuts and I know it. But so long as I make 'em laugh, they ain't going to lock me up.
  — *Red Skelton*

———

Some people have youth, some have beauty. I have menace.
  — *Edward G. Robinson*

———

I'm an artist; art has no color and no sex.
  — *Whoopi Goldberg,* the first black woman to win an Oscar in over half a century, for Best Supporting Actress in 1991's *Ghost*

Quotable Hollywood

As soon as I go out the front door of my house in the morning, I'm on, daddy, I'm on!
— *Sammy Davis Jr.*

I am just too much.
— *Bette Davis,* when asked by Barbara Walters to describe herself in five words

---

I can't play a loser. I don't look like one.
— *Rock Hudson*

I like . . . taking the big parts. I'm not interested in being worthy.
— *Anthony Hopkins*

They can't censor the gleam in my eye.
— *Charles Laughton*

I could play her better than that.
— *Julie Harris,* whispering to another actor as Queen Elizabeth approached in a reception line at Washington's Kennedy Center

Mirror, Mirror

I am simple, complex, generous, selfish, unattractive, beautiful, lazy and driven.
— *Barbra Streisand*

I have been very happy, very rich, very beautiful, much adulated, very famous and very unhappy.
— *Brigitte Bardot*

A sex symbol becomes a thing. I just hate being a thing.
— *Marilyn Monroe* in an interview published a week before her 1962 suicide

---

Being an 18-karat manic-depressive, I have an over-acute capacity for sadness as well as elation.
— *Frank Sinatra,* who also said of a Jekyll-Hyde nature, "I am a symmetrical man, almost to a fault"

I am not very interesting. But the work I do is very interesting.
— *Harrison Ford*

Quotable Hollywood

I saved Paramount . . . they were up to here in hock. By the time I was through, they were way ahead. I *saved* them, dear.
— *Mae West*

———

You don't have to manipulate me . . . [I'm not] somebody you're going to turn into a great actor so you can be the hero. I *am* a great actor.
— *James Woods,* at age 23 making his film debut in 1971's *The Visitors,* to Elia Kazan, who had directed such classics as *On the Waterfront, East of Eden,* and *A Streetcar Named Desire*

———

I've done my part for motion pictures. I've stopped making them.
— *Liberace*

———

All I have going for me is my lack of dignity.
— *Tallulah Bankhead*

———

I'm not into character assassination, except my own.
— *Carrie Fisher*

Mirror, Mirror

I used to be Snow White, but I drifted.
— *Mae West*

I never could stand my face. I dislike it thoroughly . . . It's a miracle I succeeded in the motion picture business.
— *Bette Davis*

You could put all the talent I had in your left eye and still not suffer from impaired vision.
— *Veronica Lake*

I started out as a lousy actress and have remained one.
— *Brigitte Bardot*

I have bursts of being a lady, but it doesn't last long.
— *Shelley Winters*

The thought constantly haunts me that I'm not nice enough to be doing what I am—playing a fine, idealistic young nun.
— *Sally Field* on playing Sister Bertrille in television's *The Flying Nun*

Quotable Hollywood

I could be the poster boy for bad judgment.
— *Rob Lowe*

—·—

My heart is pure as the driven slush.
— *Tallulah Bankhead*

—·—

I never know how much of what I say is true.
— *Bette Midler*

—·—

Between two evils, I always pick the one I never tried before.
— *Mae West*

—·—

If my eyes should ever turn brown, my career is shot to hell.
— *Paul Newman*, who has said "women seem more interested in my blue eyes than in anything I do or say."

—·—

You're nothing if you don't have a studio . . . Now I'm just another millionaire.
—*Jack Warner*, depressed in Palm Springs retirement

Mirror, Mirror

If I say, "This is terrible and I won't do it," go to the bank, it'll make a fortune. And anything I like goes the other way.
— *James Caan,* who reportedly rejected the lead in 1975's *One Flew Over the Cuckoo's Nest* ("it wasn't visual") and the husband in 1979's *Kramer vs. Kramer* ("middle-class horseshit")

———

As soon as people see my face on a movie screen, they know two things: First, I'm not going to get the girl, and second, I'll get a cheap funeral before the picture is over.
— *Lee Marvin*

———

Screen Gems [Studios] might not want anyone to know it, but I actually do more than sit home and chew bubble gum. I use four-letter words. I have relationships with women. I go to the bathroom—just like everyone else.
— *David Cassidy,* teenybopper idol in 1972, eager to alter his image at age 22

———

A man should control his life. Mine is controlling me.
— *Rudolph Valentino* in 1926, the year he died at age 31

Quotable Hollywood

I was a 14-year-old boy for 30 years.
— *Mickey Rooney*, who played Andy Hardy 15 times

I believe in censorship. After all, I made a fortune out of it.
— *Mae West*

I'm not a very interesting person. I haven't ever done anything except be other people.
— *Henry Fonda*

I came to Hollywood to act, not to charm society.
— *James Dean*

My nature is to be in trouble again.
— *Lauren Bacall*

I never said "I want to be alone." I only said "I want to be *let* alone." There is all the difference.
— *Greta Garbo*, setting the record straight

I cry, and I'm not ashamed of it. I think a man has to be strong to cry.
— *John Wayne*

———

Nowhere.
— *Marilyn Monroe*, listing her residence while signing the guestbook at a Malibu motel three days before her death

———

I arrived in Hollywood without having my nose fixed, my teeth capped or my name changed. That is very gratifying to me.
— *Barbra Streisand*

———

I have everything now I had 20 years ago—except now it's all lower.
— *Gypsy Rose Lee*, burlesque queen turned actress, the subject of 1962's *Gypsy*

———

I am not a sexy pot.
— *Sophia Loren*

Quotable Hollywood

I guess I'm just a sexy religious woman.
> — *Jane Russell,* answering those asking her to reconcile her
> deep religious beliefs with her roles as a screen siren

———

I was a highly sexed woman, I'll admit.
> — *Joan Crawford* to interviewer Roy Newquist

———

Dere's a millyun good-lookin' guys, but I'm a novelty.
> — *Jimmy Durante,* the nosy and lovable "Schnozzola"

———

I don't like myself, I'm *crazy* about myself.
> — *Mae West*

———

I'm the greatest comedian in the world.
> — *Frank Fay,* when asked his occupation while testifying in
> court

"What could I do?" Fay shrugged afterward. "I was under oath."

———

I won't say that I'm the best singer in the world—I'll just say I
sound better than anybody else.
> — *Al Jolson*

So They Say

So They Say

That obstinate, suspicious, egocentric, maddening, and lovable genius of a problem child.
— *Mary Pickford* on Charlie Chaplin

A Class-A bastard.
— *Liza Minnelli* on Robert De Niro

Evil.
— *Maureen O'Sullivan,* onetime actress now better known as Mia Farrow's mom, describing Woody Allen

There's nothing I wouldn't say to her face—both of them.
— *Rock Hudson* on Julie Andrews

Quotable Hollywood

Overweight, overbosomed, overpaid, and undertalented.
— *David Susskind* on Elizabeth Taylor

Get John out of the saddle and you've got trouble.
— *Joan Crawford* on John Wayne

He's got a pin-up image—which he hates. The only trouble is whenever they ask him to take his trousers off, he does.
— *Michael Caine* on Richard Gere

Impossibly self-centered, more vain than any woman I have ever met, and obsessed with sex, his penis, and conquering women.
— *Sean Young* on Warren Beatty during his bachelor days

J. C., who considers himself pretty much of a god among men . . .
— *Marilyn Beck,* Hollywood columnist, writing about Johnny Carson

---

He died at just the right time. If he had lived, he'd never have been able to live up to his publicity.
— *Humphrey Bogart* on James Dean, who died a legend at age 24 after starring in just three films

So They Say

Everybody seemed to have a lot of problems with Jimmy.
Nobody had more problems with Jimmy than Jimmy had.
— *Mercedes McCambridge,* one of the few cast members to
  befriend James Dean during the making of 1956's *Giant*

———

She was the girl every young man wanted to have—as his sister.
— *Alistair Cooke* on Mary Pickford

———

Take away Julia Roberts's wild mane of hair and all those teeth
and those elastic lips, and what've you got? A pony!
— *Joyce Haber,* columnist

———

Alec Baldwin is this big new alleged sex symbol. But he has eyes
like a weasel. He makes Clint Eastwood look like a flirt.
— *Sandy Dennis*

———

Kathleen Turner's okay in stills. When she talks and moves
about, she reminds me of someone who works in a supermarket.
— *Ann Sothern*

———

When Whoopi Goldberg wears a dress, it's like drag.
— *Mildred Natwick*

What a hamola.
— *Aldo Ray* on Charlton Heston

———

She's the original good time that was had by all.
— *Bette Davis* on Marilyn Monroe

———

It's better for Monroe not to be straightened out. The charm of her is her two left feet.
— *Billy Wilder* on Marilyn and her idiosyncrasies

———

Marilyn [Monroe] had this fantasy of having a child by Albert Einstein, whom she absolutely idolized . . . Marilyn believed that between her and Einstein, they could have the perfect child—one with her looks and his brain. By another token, what if they had a child and it had Einstein's looks and Marilyn's brain?
— *Otto Preminger*

———

She was a gigantic pain in the ass. She demonstrated certifiable proof of insanity.
— *Roman Polanski*'s quoted observation of Faye Dunaway after 1974's *Chinatown*

So They Say

He was macabre. When I was a little girl he sent me a gift of a replica of my mother [Tippi Hedren] in a coffin. That was his idea of a joke. He had a sick sense of humor.

After that, mother never worked for him again.

— *Melanie Griffith* on Alfred Hitchcock

———

Groucho I hated. I always thought he was the original dirty old man, totally insensitive.

— *Jerry Lewis,* who says he instead was influenced by Harpo, who "humanized the Marx Brothers"

———

I like Steve Allen . . . but not as much as he does.

— *Jack Paar* on his *Tonight Show* predecessor

———

He's the kind of guy that, when he dies, he's going up to Heaven and give God a bad time for making him bald.

— *Marlon Brando* on Frank Sinatra

———

I'd hate to have his nerve in my tooth.

— *Lucille Ball* on Orson Welles

Quotable Hollywood

At (D.W.) Griffith's funeral, the sacred cows of Hollywood gathered to pay him homage. A week before, he probably could not have gotten any of them on the telephone.

> — *Ezra Goodman* on the passing of the film pioneer, whose ideas were generally considered outmoded and was largely forgotten by the time of his death in 1948

———

Al Jolson's funeral was widely attended by those who wanted to make sure.

> — *George Jessel* to talkmaster Larry King

———

You look very much like Elizabeth Taylor, but you're heavier.

> — *Wife of a Mike Todd friend* upon being introduced to the 24-year-old actress before it was generally known that Taylor and Todd were keeping company

Whereupon Taylor's husband-to-be slapped her behind and said, "See, I told you you're getting fat."

So They Say

Always the bride, never the bridesmaid.
— Anonymous quote on Elizabeth Taylor Hilton Wilding Todd Fisher Burton Burton Warner Fortensky

———

He gives her class and she gives him sex.
— *Katharine Hepburn* on the dancing duo of Fred Astaire and Ginger Rogers

———

We were never screwing on stage. I never felt any sexual attraction for him . . . he's almost 50, you know.
— *Maria Schneider,* young actress, on 1973's *Last Tango in Paris* co-star Marlon Brando

———

Miss Kerr is a good actress. She also is unreasonably chaste.
— *Laurence Olivier* on Deborah Kerr

———

[Desi Arnaz] could rumba standing up and lying down.
— *People* magazine quoting a onetime "lady friend"

I knew right away that Rock Hudson was gay when he did not fall in love with me.
— *Gina Lollobrigida,* who played in two movies with Hudson in the early 1960s

---

As a director he was 10 times more wonderful than as a lover.
— *Nastassia Kinski* on Roman Polanski

He was insatiable. Three, four, five times a day was not unusual for him, and he was able to accept telephone calls at the same time.
— *Joan Collins* on Warren Beatty

I guess it was just a matter of time before she grew tired of picking up guys one at a time.
— *David Letterman* on Madonna's reported intention to buy a pro-basketball franchise

---

Better as a woman. If I were him, I'd never get out of drag.
— *Mr. Blackwell,* nee Richard Selzer, onetime struggling Hollywood actor turned self-appointed fashion critic, on Dustin Hoffman, after the star did some cross-dressing in 1982's *Tootsie*

So They Say

George C. Scott. Fine actor. Big drinker. Wife beater. What else do you want to know?
 — *Colleen Dewhurst,* actress, on the actor she married several times

———

I didn't know her well, but after watching her in action I didn't want to know her well.
 — *Joan Crawford* on Judy Garland, an MGM teammate awhile

———

An angel with spurs.
 — *Joe Pasternak* on Judy Garland

———

In spite of having the usual womanly defects, she is the only really spiritually honest woman I have ever known.
 — *Vittorio De Sica* on Sophia Loren

———

It took longer to make one of Mary's contracts than it did to make one of Mary's pictures.
 — *Samuel Goldwyn* on Pickford, whose financial shrewdness earned "America's Sweetheart" the additional nickname "The Bank of America's Sweetheart"

She'd be looking over my shoulder in the middle of a scene. I assumed she was looking at Mickey [Hargitay, her husband, who was on the set]. There was love in her eyes. Well, I snuck a glance around, and she was gazing into a full-length mirror. I couldn't believe it.

She watched herself throughout the shooting, watched herself acting. I had to have the director take the mirror away. I couldn't stand working that way.

— *Tom Ewell* on working with Jayne Mansfield for the first time

———

[Charlie] Chaplin is no businessman—all he knows is that he can't take anything less.

— *Samuel Goldwyn*

———

I'd let my wife, children, and animals starve before I'd subject myself to something like that again.

— *Don Siegel* on working with Bette Midler

———

It's amazing what a broad will do for a buck.

— *Frank Sinatra*'s reaction to onetime fellow Rat Packer Shirley MacLaine's 1995 tell-all autobiography in which he didn't fare well

So They Say

Shirley MacLaine—who does she think she *isn't*?
— *Yves Montand*

He's wanted to be Burt Lancaster all his life.
— *John Frankenheimer* on Kirk Douglas

Bogie's a hell of a nice guy until 11:30 p.m. After that he thinks he's Bogart.
— *Dave Chasen*, Hollywood restaurateur
"Bogie went around acting like Humphrey Bogart, but you got used to that after a while," noted Evelyn Keyes, once married to Bogart pal John Huston.

Oh, yeah? Well, you look like Harpo Marx!
— *Burt Reynolds* on meeting Elia Kazan, who had said, "I can't get over how much you look like Marlon Brando"

Gloria Grahame is called the girl with the novocained upper lip. Donna Reed looks like the girl with the novocained face.
— *Sonja Henie*

Quotable Hollywood

George Raft and Gary Cooper once played a scene in front of a cigar store, and it looked like the wooden Indian was overacting.
> — *George Burns*

———

He's the sort of guy if you say, "Hiya, Clark, how are ya?" he's stuck for an answer.
> —*Ava Gardner* describing fellow actor, pal, and onetime lover Clark Gable—a crack that made even Gable laugh

———

I just don't know what the hell he's after.
> — *Frank Capra* on Ingmar Bergman

———

To Raoul Walsh, a tender love scene is burning down a whorehouse.
> —*Jack Warner* on the veteran director, who featured action over dialogue

———

Steven Spielberg always wanted to be a little boy when he grew up.
> — *Rainer Werner Fassbinder* on a fellow director

So They Say

If there were a way to make movies without actors, George would do it.
— *Mark Hamill,* after making 1977's *Star Wars* for George Lucas

---

If I'm ever stupid enough to be caught working with you again, you'll know that I'm either broke or I've lost my mind.
— *Cary Grant* to Michael Curtiz upon completion of 1946's *Night and Day*—Grant disliking his performance in the film, but not as much as he despised its director

---

Otto [Preminger] is a dear man—sort of a Jewish Nazi, but I love him . . .
— *Joan Crawford*

[Montgomery Clift] was an exceptionally bright man who liked to pretend he wasn't—unlike Marlon Brando who likes to pretend he's bright, whereas in fact he isn't very.
— *Edward Dmytryk,* who directed both actors in 1958's *The Young Lions*

She transcends all boundaries; she's a totally sincere actress, and at once a bitch and man's best friend. With gorgeous hair, yet.
— *Patsy Kelly* on fellow actress Lassie, whom she called "the most beautiful female star in filmdom"

I really liked Lassie, but that horse Flicka was a nasty animal with a terrible disposition. All the Flickas—all six of them—were awful.
— *Roddy McDowall,* teen star of 1943's *Lassie Come Home* and *My Friend Flicka*

She's a legend, but once you get beyond that, she's just a cranky old broad who can sometimes be a whole lot of fun.
— *Nick Nolte* on Katharine Hepburn after they starred in 1984's *The Ultimate Solution of Grace Quigley*

I'm not nearly as cranky as I should have been with him . . . He was getting drunk in every gutter in town.
— *Katharine Hepburn* responding to Nick Nolte

Yes, [Wallace] Beery is a son of a bitch. But he's *our* son of a bitch.
　　— *Louis B. Mayer,* (sort of) defending one of MGM's cantankerous star actors

———

Which is he playing now?
　　— *Somerset Maugham,* while observing Spencer Tracy on 1941's *Dr. Jekyll and Mr. Hyde* set

———

Robert De Niro is a very intense actor. He doesn't play joy very well.
　　— *Neil Simon,* explaining why the actor, trying comedy, was out of Simon's 1977 movie *The Goodbye Girl* two weeks into filming

———

She'd be better off if she spent more time learning her lines and less time reciting her rosary.
　　— *William Holden* on *Picnic* (1955) co-star Kim Novak, who, nervous at her first starring opportunity, reportedly prayed nightly in a Catholic church while on location in Kansas

Quotable Hollywood

She was good at playing abstract confusion in the same way that a midget is good at being short.
— *Clive James,* critic, commenting on Marilyn Monroe's acting

When I can't sleep I read a book by Steve Allen.
— *Oscar Levant*

The weirdest man you ever want to work with.
— *Virginia Mayo* on Jack Palance

Yes, I have acted with Clint Eastwood. Or, rather, I have acted opposite Clint Eastwood.
— *Geraldine Page*

Acting with [Laurence] Harvey is like acting by yourself—only worse.
— *Jane Fonda* on her co-star in 1962's *A Walk on the Wild Side*

I gave up being serious about making pictures around the time I made a film with Greer Garson and she took 125 takes to say no.
— *Robert Mitchum,* recalling working on 1947's *Desire Me*

So They Say

Errol Flynn always said he knew nothing about acting, and I admired his honesty because he was absolutely right.
— *Bette Davis* on her *one*-time co-star
Davis so disliked Flynn that she reportedly turned down the role of Scarlett O'Hara in Gone with the Wind *because she thought Flynn was being cast to co-star as Rhett Butler.*

All right . . . if you don't mind a dozen takes.
— *Humphrey Bogart* on the acting ability of Audrey Hepburn, his young co-star in 1954's *Sabrina*

I must say I haven't noticed any improvement, however, since she took those elaborate acting lessons. I have always said she should have gone to a train engineer's school instead to learn something about arriving on schedule.
— *Billy Wilder* on Marilyn Monroe's lessons at the Actors Studio—and about her notorious habit of being late

It's not really me that's late. It's the others that are in such a hurry.
— *Marilyn Monroe* responding to Billy Wilder

Quotable Hollywood

Honey, I've had it. Go get yours. It's your turn now.
— *Betty Grable,* turning over the spotlight as the blonde queen of 20th Century-Fox to Marilyn Monroe in the mid-Fifties

When Mumbles is through rehearsing, I'll come out.
— *Frank Sinatra,* a one-take actor, to Joe Mankiewicz, referring to 25-take Marlon Brando during 1955's *Guys and Dolls* filming

Most of the time he sounds like he has a mouth full of wet toilet paper.
— *Rex Reed* on Marlon Brando

There is not enough money in Hollywood to lure me into making another picture with Joan Crawford. And I like money.
— *Sterling Hayden* on his 1954's *Johnny Guitar* co-star

Dramatic art in her opinion is knowing how to fill a sweater.
— *Bette Davis* on Jayne Mansfield

So They Say

I gave Anthony Perkins his first big break. But don't blame me—that's Hollywood, folks!
— *George Cukor*

—·—

Joan Collins is to acting what her sister Jackie is to English literature.
— *London Daily Express*

—·—

Like cracking the whip at a limping horse.
— *Franco Zeffirelli* on directing Brooke Shields

—·—

Ginger Rogers did everything that Fred Astaire did. She just did it backwards and in high heels.
— Variously attributed to Linda Ellerbee and others

—·—

Until this spun-sugar zombie melts from our screen, there is little chance of American film's coming of age.
— *John Simon* on Doris Day

"The only real talent Miss Day possesses," the British critic wrote, "is that of being absolutely sanitary: her personality untouched by human emotion, her brow unclouded by human thought, her form unsmudged by the slightest evidence of femininity . . ."

Quotable Hollywood

If Roseanne Barr is the new Lucille Ball, I'm the new Garbo.
— *Nancy Walker*

—·—

Bob Hope is still about as funny as he ever was. I just never thought he was that funny in the first place.
— *Chevy Chase* during the Eighties

—·—

Gable's an idiot. You know why he's an actor? It's the only thing he's smart enough to do.
— *John Wayne* on Clark Gable

—·—

I'd love to work with her again, in something appropriate. Perhaps *Macbeth*.
— *Walter Matthau* on Barbra Streisand after their warfare during the making of 1969's *Hello Dolly!*

—·—

What the hell would a bald-headed old son of a bitch like you know about hair lashing across your eyes?
— *Maureen O'Hara* erupting at John Ford during filming of 1952's *The Quiet Man*—when the director chided the actress for blinking while her fan-whipped hair "was lashing across my eyes like pieces of steel" during the horse-race scene

So They Say

She looked as though butter wouldn't melt in her mouth—or anywhere else.
— *Elsa Lanchester* on Maureen O'Hara

I followed her instructions. I slapped her so you could hear it all over the set. And the cast and crew burst into applause.
— *Edward G. Robinson,* recalling a scene with Miriam Hopkins in 1935's *Barbary Coast*

I can't imagine Rhett Butler chasing you for 10 years.
— *David O. Selznick*'s alleged response to Katharine Hepburn's reported appeal for the female lead in *Gone with the Wind*

Dyan Cannon . . . looks a bit like Lauren Bacall and a bit like Jeanne Moreau, but the wrong bits . . .
— *Pauline Kael,* writing about 1969's *Bob & Carol & Ted & Alice*

If her household runs as perfectly as her press would have us believe, I'll slash my throat.
— *Susan Sarandon* on Meryl Streep

Richard Gere and Cindy Crawford—he's elastic and she's plastic.
— *Sandra Bernhard*
Comedian Sam Kinison also had something to say about the two: "Such a pair, and what a concept—his body's by Nautilus and her mind's by Mattel."

It's too bad they don't have voice-lifts.
— *Dame Judith Anderson* on James Stewart
"Jimmy Stewart's voice was barely tolerable when he was young," said the stage actress, who made more than two-dozen films into her mid-80s and lived into her 90s. "Now it's a trial to listen to.
"Fortunately, he never has anything interesting to say."

You're so lucky not to be a big Hollywood star, bound to a contract.
— *Joan Fontaine* to Celeste Holm, who, Fontaine noted, "is cool to me to this day"

Will Star
Joe Star
John Star
Jed Star
Jim Star
Joan Star
Jack Star

It's All Relative

It's All Relative

---•---

She has only two things going for her—a father and a mother.
   — *John Simon* on Liza Minnelli, Vincente and Judy's daughter

---

My daddy is a movie actor, and sometimes he plays the good guy and sometimes he plays the lawyer.
   — *Malcolm Ford*, explaining to pre-school mates what his father Harrison does for a living

---

Being a dumb blonde must run in that family.
   — *Derek Jarman*, British director and screenwriter, while skewering Melanie Griffith, daughter of Tippi Hedren

Professionally, we got along just fine. It was living with him that was the bitch.

— *Peter Douglas*, Kirk's producer son

Wouldn't you be insecure if she were your aunt? I saw her last Christmas, and she told me that I have no muscle tone in my thighs.

— *Bridget Fonda* on her physically fit Auntie Jane

I'd love to do a love scene with him just to see what all the yelling is about.

— *Shirley MacLaine* on baby brother Warren Beatty

Connie, funny thing, your kids look just like *my* kids.

— *Debbie Reynolds* to Connie Stevens, both formerly Mrs. Eddie Fisher (and Liz Taylor makes three)—as quoted by columnist Earl Wilson

I don't expect to hear from him on my birthday or Christmas. I see him when I see him. He's like a ghost. And that's cool.

— *Jamie Lee Curtis* on dad Tony Curtis

It's All Relative

Take 'em down to Grauman's Chinese [Theater] and show 'em where they pushed your grandfather's face in it.
— *John Drew Barrymore's* suggestion to his son when John Blyth Barrymore called to say he was in jail for walking on wet cement

———

You can't be a movie star. Movie stars are beautiful.
— *Debra Winger's* father, reacting to news that she was dropping out of college to pursue acting
Undaunted, she replied, "Okay, then I'll be an actress."

———

No, but I gained a father.
— *Robert Taylor,* when asked if he'd gotten the raise he sought from Louis B. Mayer—the MGM mogul telling the actor that he was like the son he never had, and had big plans for him . . . but no money

———

Sparkle, Shirley, sparkle!
— *Gertrude Temple,* Shirley's mother, standing just off camera as usual
"I soon learned not to let my affections make me too lenient," noted the ambitious Mrs. Temple, who each night drilled her daughter on the next day's lines.

Quotable Hollywood

Just imagine what you could accomplish if you tried celibacy.
— *Shirley MacLaine* to "my dear, sweet, talented brother"
   Warren Beatty during the 1978 Academy Awards cere-
   monies—big sister on stage as presenter, little brother in
   the audience awaiting word on his four *Heaven Can Wait*
   nominations

I've always followed my father's advice: He told me to never
insult anybody unintentionally. So if I insult you, you can be
goddamn sure I intend to.
— *John Wayne*

Love
&
Marriage

Love & Marriage

My advice to most any man in this business is, don't marry an actress, and I know whereof I speak.
— *Henry Fonda*

Chapter XXVIII: My Marriage to Ernest Borgnine
[Remainder of page—and chapter—blank]
— *Ethel Merman*'s chapter in her autobiography on the singer's 38-day marriage to the actor

You know, Mick, I'm god-damned tired of living with a midget.
— *Ava Gardner*'s reported last words to Mickey Rooney before leaving him

We couldn't live together and we couldn't live apart.
  — *George C. Scott*'s explanation of his multiple marriages
    and divorces with/from Colleen Dewhurst

———

She has a double chin and an overdeveloped chest and she's
rather short in the leg. So I can hardly describe her as the most
beautiful creature I've ever seen.
  — *Richard Burton* on Elizabeth Taylor, whom he married
    twice

———

Desi is a loser. A gambler, an alcoholic, a skirt-chaser . . . a
financially smart man but self-destructive. He's just a loser.
  — *Lucille Ball* on Desi Arnaz

———

She has a big comic talent, but she also has a big, not very funny
temper. Not a temperament but a *temper*. Her tongue is her
lethal weapon. She can be cruel when she wants to be.
  — *Desi* on Lucy

———

[There's a rumor] I made Esther give up her career when we got
married. That's a lie. She was already washed up when we got
married.
  — *Fernando Lamas* on Esther Williams

Marlon is now balding, paunchy. He remains an iconoclast without icons, a Messiah without a god. He is a genius without taste. He is a frightened, lonely child.
— *Anna Kashfi* on former husband Marlon Brando

———

Listen, buddy, I only *play* the Terminator—you married one.
— *Arnold Schwarzenegger* to Tom Arnold, referring to Roseanne

———

Who do you think you are, my husband?
— *Ingrid Bergman* to Roberto Rossellini, later recalling, "When he would bark an order at me, sometimes I would forget we were married and shout [that] back"

———

She wanted us to be like brother and sister. But, fortunately, occasional incest was allowed.
— *Laurence Olivier* on Vivien Leigh

———

Dixie, don't marry that bum. If you do, you'll have to support him for the rest of your life.
— *Sol Wurtzel,* a Fox boss, to rising star Dixie Lee, warning against her 1930 marriage to a young crooner named Bing Crosby

Quotable Hollywood

Let's stop fighting, Artie. People will think we're still married.
— *Ava Gardner* to Artie Shaw, capping a loud argument
when the onetime mates attended a concert together long
after their stormy marriage

She chooses to forget that I was her first. Husband, that is.
— *Richard Cromwell,* actor, on Angela Lansbury

It was a love-hate affair. At times he loved me as much as I
hated him.
— *Greta Garbo* on Swedish director Mauritz Stiller, her
mentor

Dennis Quaid and Meg Ryan are expecting a child in March.
And get this—they're even married!
— *Liz Smith,* columnist

I have a steak at home. Why should I go out for a hamburger?
— *Paul Newman* on Joanne Woodward, married since 1958

Love & Marriage

Who would marry Rita for her cooking?
  — *Dick Haymes,* when asked at his wedding to Rita
    Hayworth if she had ever cooked for him

———

When he's late for dinner, I know he's either having an affair or
is lying dead in the street. I always hope it's the street.
  — *Jessica Tandy* on actor/husband Hume Cronyn

———

I love Mickey Mouse more than any woman I've ever known.
  — *Walt Disney*

———

The trouble with some women is that they get all excited about
nothing—and then marry him.
  — *Cher*

———

Marriage is the best magician there is. In front of your eyes it
can change an exciting, cute little dish into a boring dishwasher.
  — *Ryan O'Neal*

———

Take it from me: Marriage isn't a word, it's a sentence.
  — *King Vidor*

Marriage is a great institution, but I'm not ready for an institution.
— *Mae West*

———

I'd rather be dead than wed.
— *Cybill Shepherd*

———

They say marriages are made in heaven. So are thunder and lightning.
— *Clint Eastwood*

———

Communication—and separate bedrooms and separate bathrooms.
— *Bette Davis,* wed four times, suggesting the most crucial elements in marriage

———

It's easy to do with 2,000 different girls. What's hard is 2,000 times with your wife.
— *George Burns* to Walter Matthau's "I heard there's a book out that says Hugh Hefner has had 2,000 women in 20 years."

Love & Marriage

I'd marry again if I found a man who had $15 million and would sign over half of it to me before the marriage and guarantee he'd be dead within a year.
— *Bette Davis* after four marriages and a near-miss, when Nearly Number 5 fled rather than sign a prenuptial agreement

———

Many a man owes his success to his first wife and his second wife to his success.
— *Jim Backus*

———

It's an extra dividend when you like the girl you're in love with.
— *Clark Gable*

———

Next to privacy, the rarest thing in Hollywood is a wedding anniversary.
— *Gene Fowler,* journalist and screenwriter

———

I know a lot of people didn't expect our relationship to last, but we've just celebrated our two-months' anniversary.
— *Britt Ekland*

Quotable Hollywood

I don't care if she doesn't know how to cook—so long as she doesn't know a good lawyer.
— *Errol Flynn,* defining his ideal wife

———

I have never hated a man enough to give his diamonds back.
— *Zsa Zsa Gabor*

———

I've had far too many affairs to think of myself as a normal, rational man.
— *Marlon Brando*

———

My love life is what's important to me. That's number one, even before acting.
— *Al Pacino*

———

I sold my memoirs of my love life to Parker Brothers and they are going to make a game out of it.
— *Woody Allen* before a more recent chapter

As long as [men] serve my purpose, they're fine. But if they take up too much of my time, I eliminate them—see what I mean? I'm not going to stop being Mae West for any man.

— *Mae West*, a celebrated "man-eater," who "didn't want no husband because he'd of interfered with my hobby and my career"

———

None of my four husbands was man enough to become Mr. Bette Davis.

— *Ms. Bette Davis*

———

I've only slept with the men I've been married to. How many women can make that claim?

— *Elizabeth Taylor*, wed eight times (albeit twice to the same man, Richard Burton)

The Naked Truth

The Naked Truth

—————◆—————

Procreation is nature's principle occupation, and every man, whether he be young or old, when meeting any woman, measures the potentiality of sex between them. Thus it has always been with me.
  — *Charlie Chaplin,* who spoke from long and sometimes controversial experience

—————

Sex must be in the face, not the body . . . If you have to show your body, then you haven't got it, dear.
  — *Mae West*

—————

Sex appeal is 50 percent what you've got and 50 percent what people *think* you've got.
  — *Sophia Loren*

Oh, yeah.
> — *George Burns,* just before his 100th birthday, when asked
> by Carol Channing if he sensed his sex appeal

Being baldpate is an unfailing sex magnet.
> — *Telly Savalas*

I don't believe that I have any of this sex appeal that you hear all
the women talk about. As many a disappointed young lady will
tell you, I'm a lousy lover.
> — *Clark Gable*

*"To tell the truth," wife Carole Lombard once agreed, "he isn't such a
hell of a good lay."*

People think I have a sexy walk. Hell, I'm just trying to hold my
gut in.
> — *Robert Mitchum*

Once they call you a "Latin lover" you're in real trouble. Women
expect an Oscar performance in bed.
> — *Marcello Mastroianni*

The Naked Truth

Being a sex symbol was rather like being a convict.
— *Raquel Welch*

———

In his heyday [Howard] Hughes boasted of deflowering 200 virgins in Hollywood. He must have got them all.
— *Jimmy "The Greek" Snyder* on a fellow Las Vegan

———

What a wonderful display of beautiful women, and I've had every one of them.
— *Clark Gable* as he scanned a publicity photo of MGM's female stars

———

There was never any trouble getting girls. But it's big trouble getting rid of them.
— *Sean Connery,* quoted by Sheilah Graham during his younger days

———

I swear Gene is the only person I have ever slept with to get a part in a movie.
— *Gilda Radner,* recalling making 1986's *Haunted Honeymoon* for/with director/co-star Gene Wilder, her husband

Nobody ever objected to Botticelli's Venus, so why should they object to my posing in the nude?
— *Marilyn Monroe*

———

I just don't feel that my algebra teacher should ever know what my butt looks like.
— *Julia Roberts*, explaining why she refuses to do nude scenes

———

Honey, I thought you'd like to see the beautiful body you're going to have the opportunity of dressing.
— *Mae West*, making her entrance to meet costume designer Walter Plunkett for the first time—clad only in high heels and a long wig

———

Silly, that's the way I was born and that's the way I sleep.
— *Gloria Grahame*, when asked by Rex Reed about being "obviously starkers under the sheets" during 1950's *In a Lonely Place*, reportedly a movie first

———

I could stand nude in the middle of Madison Square Garden now and I don't think it would faze me.
— *Sharon Stone*

The Naked Truth

You would think all other women kept their bodies in vaults.
— *Marilyn Monroe* after sparking a controversy by wearing a
low-cut, clinging dress in 1952

I wish someone *would* ask me to take off my clothes.
— *Sally Field* at age 48 in 1995, while telling a college
drama seminar that being asked to do a nude scene
wouldn't bother her as long as it fit naturally into the story

---

To err is human, but it feels divine.
— *Mae West*

The good die young—because they see it's no use living if
you've got to be good.
— *John Barrymore*

Sex is emotion in motion.
— *Mae West*

Doing love scenes with Clark Gable [in *Gone with the Wind*]
was not that romantic. His dentures smelled something awful.
— *Vivien Leigh*

[He] preferred making spaghetti . . . to making love.
— *Pola Negri* on Rudolph Valentino

———

Sex: The thing that takes up the least amount of time and causes the most amount of trouble.
— *John Barrymore*

———

The only difference between sex and death is, with death you can do it alone and nobody's going to make fun of you.
— *Woody Allen*

I'll Drink
to That

I'll Drink to That

The trouble with the world is that it's always one drink behind.
— *Humphrey Bogart*

"Hair Tonic" . . . "Skin Freshener" . . . "Cleansers" . . .
— *Errol Flynn*'s labels, among others, on various bottles in his studio makeup man's kit—camouflaging a variety of beverages the actor kept handy on the set

Anyone who stayed drunk for 25 years as I did would have to be in trouble. Hell, I used to take two-week lunch hours.
— *Spencer Tracy*

Quotable Hollywood

I got Mark Hellinger so drunk last night that it took three bell-boys to put me to bed.
> — *W. C. Fields,* an all-world booze-ster, admiring the drinking capacity of the Broadway columnist/Hollywood producer

———

John, if you weren't the son of my beloved friend [Walter Huston], and if you weren't a brilliant writer, a fine actor and a magnificent director—you'd be nothing but a common drunk.
> — *Gregory Ratoff,* director

———

Yes, I have a drinking problem. You [interviewer Roy Newquist] know I have a drinking problem, and maybe you have, too—you've matched me drink for drink for years . . .
> — *Joan Crawford*

———

One more drink and I'll be under the host.
> — *Dorothy Parker*

———

Because it doesn't give you a hangover. You may get some broken ribs and broken legs from falling down, but no hangover.
> — *John Wayne,* explaining why "I like tequila."

I'll Drink to That

Drink, drink, drink. Smoke, smoke, smoke. Schmuck, schmuck, schmuck.
> — *Frank Sinatra,* miserable and raspily chastising himself during a television taping break after partying strenuously the night before

———

That was the only time I've ever got a hangover from just listening.
> — *Jack Paar* to his *Tonight Show* audience following a disastrous interview with a tipsy Mickey Rooney

———

Some son of a bitch put pineapple juice in my pineapple juice.
> — *W. C. Fields,* after studio officials, trying to keep him sober, secretly replaced his gin-laced juice with plain juice

———

Fire gets you sober real quick.
> — *Richard Pryor,* recalling setting himself on fire

———

My body, my liver [were] okay; my brain went.
> — *Dennis Hopper,* who noted, "I was lucky to get out of the Seventies alive."

Quotable Hollywood

I don't miss waking up next to the ugliest girls in the world.
— *Richard Harris*, listing for interviewer Roger Ebert a benefit of swearing off booze

———

Drinking makes such fools of people, and people are such fools to begin with, that it's compounding a felony.
— *Robert Benchley*

Whatever You Say

Whatever You Say

What's left of her.
— *Tallulah Bankhead*, when someone asked if she was "the famous Tallulah"

Former actor.
— *Robert Mitchum*, when asked his occupation while being booked at a Los Angeles jail for possession of marijuana in 1948

We hate Lucy.
— What *Lucille Ball* feared critics might say about her new comedy series when the title *I Love Lucy* was proposed prior to airing on CBS in October 1951

Quotable Hollywood

Joe, Joe. You never heard such cheering.
> — *Marilyn Monroe* to Joe DiMaggio, after the bride returned from a sidetrip to entertain U.S. troops in Korea during their Japanese honeymoon

Yes, I did.
> — *Joe DiMaggio*, in response to Marilyn Monroe

———

I am *now!*
> — *Rosie O'Donnell* to another female customer in a store, who had said, "Hope you're not insulted, but you look just like Rosie O'Donnell."

———

My grunt.
> —*Johnny Weissmuller*, when asked the secret of his success as a Hollywood Tarzan

———

Frank who?
> — *Howard Hughes*, while refusing to take phone calls from a longtime adversary named Sinatra

Whatever You Say

I just can't sit next to somebody for nearly half an hour and not say hello.
> — *Edward G. Robinson* to Charlton Heston, breaking the long silence as the actors were side by side waiting for the crew to set up a scene

Well, I can.
> — *Charlton Heston,* reportedly responding to Edward G. Robinson

———

Promises, promises.
> — *Dorothy Parker,* while hospitalized for alcoholism, responding to a doctor's warning that she'd soon be dead if she didn't quit drinking

———

Only nuts are interesting people.
> — *Roman Polanski,* reportedly explaining why he had cast 23-year-old Mia Farrow with her "neurotic quality" as the female lead in 1968's *Rosemary's Baby*

———

Because she doesn't wear underwear.
> — *Bob Mackie,* the fashion designer, explaining why he didn't name something in his new lingerie line for star customer Cher

Because you can arrive on the set with dirty, stringy hair. You don't have to look pretty and well-groomed to direct.
— *Penny Marshall* on why she prefers directing to acting

———

I found I could be popular with young ladies if I could dance.
— *Gene Kelly* on why he began dancing

———

I'm not crazy about the stuff. But money is money.
— *Macaulay Culkin* explaining why he signed a fat contract to endorse Sprite™

———

To pay for my American Express.™
— *Peter Ustinov* on why he made a commercial for American Express™

———

If you're a young blonde around this man's town, you have to keep the wolf pack off somehow. If you know all those words, they figure you know your way around and they don't act quite so rough.

It's better than having a blacksnake whip in your hand.
— *Carole Lombard* on why she used profanity freely

Whatever You Say

I did not want to be known as Kate Smith.
— *Katharine Hepburn* on why she divorced Ludlow
    Ogden Smith

There is only one Joan Crawford.
— *Joan Crawford,* replying to actor Scott Brady, who found
    her autographing a stack of fan mail and asked why she
    didn't let a secretary sign her name

Mostly, I didn't want to be poor.
— *Bette Midler* on why she turned to singing when her early
    acting efforts were unsuccessful

Yeah, sure, Quentin—but how about before my teeth fall out
and my breasts sag?
— *Pam Grier* to Quentin Tarantino, when he reiterated that
    he was writing a movie for her—a two-year project that
    would result in 1997's *Jackie Brown*

I'm very stunned and flattered and glad to learn that the rest of
Mr. Will's body is not as conservative as his brain.
— *Susan Sarandon*'s reaction to making columnist George
    Will's list of what he would like to take to another planet

Quotable Hollywood

I thought they'd make me gorgeous. I always wanted to be pretty.

> — *Barbra Streisand,* expressing disappointment to *Look* magazine on how she looked on the big screen in her movie debut, 1968's *Funny Girl,* for which she won an Oscar

I've always wanted to shake the hand that patted Lana Turner's ass.

> — A grinning commanding officer outside a Navy boot-camp barracks, extending a "put-'er-there" handshake to a recruit named Artie Shaw, who had been married to the movie queen

What on earth for?

> — *Miriam Hopkins* to escort Richard Higham, when he informed her that he was writing a biography of Cecil B. DeMille

It was another actress who accused me. My answer to that is, quote: Those who know me better know better. That's all. Unquote.

> — *Marilyn Monroe,* countering an allegation that she wore falsies

120

Whatever You Say

Pardon me, ma'am. I thought you were a guy I knew in Pittsburgh.
> — *Groucho Marx* to Greta Garbo after he'd reportedly
> peeked under her hat brim and was greeted with an icy
> stare

Bitchery, dear. Sheer bitchery.
> — *Hedda Hopper,* responding to Merle Oberon's demand to
> know why the gossip columnist had written malicious
> things about her

I've had a wonderful evening—but this wasn't it.
> — *Groucho Marx* to a Hollywood hostess

With the crown of thorns I wear, why should I be bothered with
a prick like you?
> — *Dorothy Parker* to a drunk who was bothering her at a bar
> during the Hollywood blacklisting of the late-Forties

Quotable Hollywood

Oh, yes. Did you come?
  — *Ethel Barrymore,* responding to a young actress who, after
    ignoring an invitation, said lamely during a chance meet-
    ing a few days later, "I think I was invited to your house to
    dinner last Thursday night."

———

Thanks anyway, Audrey.
  — Stranger to Katharine Hepburn as he walked away after
    being refused an autograph in Central Park by the actress,
    who rarely signs

———

Apparently somewhere before Christ.
  — *Charlton Heston,* whose Biblical roles ranged from Moses
    to John the Baptist, when asked to which historical era his
    face belonged

———

What the hell am I supposed to do, play Bogart?
  — *Spencer Tracy,* when accused of always playing himself

———

I do all of my best work in bed.
  — *Mae West,* queen of the double entendre, when asked how
    she wrote her memoirs

Whatever You Say

Lots of grapefruit throughout the day and plenty of virile young men.
> — *Angie Dickinson,* revealing "my diet secret"

I'd just like to be remembered.
> — *Jackie Gleason,* when asked by columnist Pete Hamill how he'd like to be remembered

Someone peculiar.
> — *Bette Davis,* during a Q&A with a Pasadena theater audience, when asked who should play her in a Bette Davis film biography

I'd live over a saloon.
> — *W. C. Fields,* when asked what he'd do differently if he had his life to live over

It was horrible and I hated it.
> — *Kirsten Dunst,* age 12, reacting to kissing teen heartthrob Brad Pitt in 1994's *Interview with the Vampire*

All the years I owned RKO, I *never* once set foot inside the place.

> — *Howard Hughes,* correcting a popular Hollywood story that the eccentric billionaire had visited *once*—dropping by around midnight soon after buying the studio and ordering simply, "Paint it"

No, darling. Have you?

> — *Tallulah Bankhead,* deep-voiced actress, responding to columnist Earl Wilson's "Have you ever been mistaken for a man?"

I walked. I didn't have the carfare.

> — *Al Pacino,* native New Yorker, giving a smart-ass, on-air response to what he considered a vacuous question by Merv Griffin, "So how did you get from the Bronx to Broadway?"

My era will end the day they put me in my grave.

> — *Bette Davis,* testily, to a young actress who asked, "Miss Davis, back in your era, what was it like in Hollywood?"

Whatever You Say

Congratulations, Mr. Arnaz. You are the only man who has ever screwed his wife, Cecil B. DeMille, Paramount Pictures, and Harry Cohn—all at the same time.

> — *Cecil B. DeMille* to Desi Arnaz, after wife Lucille Ball revealed she was pregnant—thus wiping out Columbia's plans to loan her to Paramount to star in 1952's *The Greatest Show on Earth*

———

Yes, but what about the deaf ones?

> — *Katharine Hepburn* to John Huston, after the director assured the actress that he had scared off crocodiles with rifle-fire noise before she entered the water during location filming of 1951's *The African Queen*

———

Don't be nervous, but don't make any mistakes.

> — *Fred Astaire*'s advice to dancing partner Barrie Chase before they did a number, as recalled by Chase

———

Let the heathen drown!

> — *Mary Pickford* to husband Douglas Fairbanks, who had jumped into their Pickfair pool fully clothed to rescue a gasping Charlie Chaplin, an atheist who had punctuated a debate on religion by leaping into the water and yelling, "If there's a god, let Him save me!"

I'm paid to shout at you!
— *Ernst Lubitsch*'s bellowed response to Gene Tierney's
near-tears complaint that the director was continually
yelling at her during filming of 1943's *Heaven Can Wait*
*"And I'm paid to take it—but not enough!" fired back the actress, who
was mad as hell and wouldn't take it any more.*

*After a tense pause, Tierney once recalled, "Lubitsch broke out
laughing. From then on we got along famously."*

———

This is a movie, chowderhead, not a lifeboat.
— *Spencer Tracy* to Garson Kanin, who had asked why the
actor always had top billing over frequent co-star
Katharine Hepburn—always Tracy and Hepburn, in that
order—and why not "ladies first"?

———

What are you going to do, talk the alien to death?
— *James Cameron*'s response to Sigourney Weaver's hesitancy
about using guns in 1986 hit *Aliens*

———

Because I don't like you.
— *Lana Turner*, replying to Hedda Hopper's "Why can't we
be friends?"

Sorry, I cannot do your picture. I have more important things to do.
> — *Shelley Winters,* "barely polite" in rejecting director Fred Zinnemann's offer of the role of the prostitute in *From Here to Eternity*, 1953's Best Picture

"So Donna Reed got that (Best Supporting) Oscar," regretted Winters, who turned down the role because she was angry at Hollywood at the time.

Ah, get yourself a chair, Katie, and pull up one for me. And fix the drinks.
> — *Humphrey Bogart,* needling co-star Katharine Hepburn on *The African Queen* location, where she continually lectured Bogart and director John Huston on the evils of whisky

Yes, Mr. Gable. What do you do?
> — *William Faulkner,* when the novelist came to Hollywood to do some screenwriting for MGM and was asked by Clark Gable: "Do you write?"

Dottie, if you don't stop this sort of thing you'll make yourself sick.

 — *Robert Benchley* to longtime associate Dorothy Parker after one of her suicide attempts

———

If you played both parts, how would you know which queen to upstage?

 — *John Carradine* to Katharine Hepburn, who, according to Carradine, had said she really wanted to play both Elizabeth and Mary in 1936's *Mary of Scotland*

———

Tell the son of a bitch we're on schedule.

 — *John Ford,* tearing out the next six pages of script, after a messenger delivered an advisory from the studio's head noting that filming was two days behind schedule

Frank Sinatra said and did much the same when an assistant director interrupted the actor's afternoon "martini time" break during filming of 1958's Some Came Running *and claimed that production was behind schedule.*

"How far behind are we?" Sinatra asked.

"Two weeks," replied the assistant.

Sinatra ripped out about 20 pages from the script, according to Shirley MacLaine, who was there earning an Oscar nomination as the female lead.

"There, pal," Sinatra said. "Now we're on schedule."

Whatever You Say

I'm sure you know what a whore looks like if anyone does.
  — *Carole Lombard* to Harry Cohn's "Your hair's too
  white . . . you look like a whore."

———

If you don't, they'll think you're a pansy.
  — *Howard Hughes* to Robert Mitchum, who while filming
  1951's *My Forbidden Past* reportedly phoned the RKO
  boss and asked—regarding Hughes's onetime girl friend
  Ava Gardner—"Do you mind if I go to bed with her?"

———

Don't worry, Miss Hepburn. I'll cut you down to my size.
  — *Spencer Tracy*'s alleged response to Katharine Hepburn's
  also alleged "I'm afraid I am a little tall for you, Mr. Tracy"
  at their first meeting before filming began on 1942's
  Woman of the Year, the first of their many movies
  together—a flinty start to their lifelong relationship

———

Let's get a baby carriage, Ruthie, and you and I wheel it up
South Water Street.
  — *Mia Farrow* to Ruth Gordon on Martha's Vineyard—
  soon after they had starred in 1968's *Rosemary's Baby*

Quotable Hollywood

In a *horizontal* position?
> — *Shelley Winters,* screaming at new husband Anthony Franciosa, who had protested he was "only helping" Anna Magnani "with her English" when Winters discovered them "stretched out, kissing" (albeit with scripts in hand) on a living-room couch in a Hollywood penthouse

So will yours when I get through with you.
> — *Robert Mitchum* to a producer who was scrutinizing the young actor (a onetime professional boxer) for a part— finding one fault after another, including, "My God, man, your nose is broken!"

SIGN BEFORE THEY CHANGE THEIR MINDS.
> — *Ronald Reagan*'s 1937 cable to agent Bill Meiklejohn, as the 26-year-old Iowa sportscaster accepted Warner Brothers' $200-a-week offer

You tell him it's his co-star from *The Winning Team.* I was married to him when he was only Grover Cleveland Alexander the baseball player, and he'd better call me back if he knows what's good for him.
> — *Doris Day,* calling California Governor Ronald Reagan to ask his help in animal rights

Whatever You Say

We will resume shooting, Miss Hepburn, when the Directors Guild card which I ordered for you arrives.

— *Joseph Mankiewicz,* directing Katharine Hepburn (reportedly yelling) as they warred while filming 1959's *Suddenly, Last Summer*

Hepburn reportedly celebrated the conclusion of the troubled production by spitting in Mankiewicz's face.

———

FORGET ME. (Signed) GLORIA.

— *Gloria Swanson*'s cable from Paris to Marshall "Mickey" Neilan, ending their high-voltage romance—to which Neilan wired back:

FORGOTTEN. (Signed) MICKEY.

———

DO WE SAY DON'T GO TO SEE LAUREN BACALL MOVIES?

— American Floral Association's telegram to widow Lauren Bacall, who, upon Humphrey Bogart's death, had invited contributions to the American Cancer Society in lieu of flowers

Bacall received the wire when she and a houseful of guests returned from the funeral service for a final toast to Bogie.

"That gave me and all who saw it the one true laugh of the day," the actress wrote in Lauren Bacall By Myself.

Quotable Hollywood

You may not have a hole in your windpipe but we love you anyway.
> — *Billy Wilder*'s telegram to Shirley MacLaine in Japan when she lost 1960's Best Actress Oscar to Elizabeth Taylor, who'd had a tracheotomy while surviving a recent brush with death

———

Practice, practice!
> — Inscription scrawled on an eye chart sent by Frank Sinatra to pal Sammy Davis Jr. after the entertainer lost an eye in a 1954 auto accident

———

Dear sir: Send her to the dry cleaners.
> — *Alfred Hitchcock*, replying to a letter that stated, "My daughter, after seeing the French film *Diabolique*, would never use the bathtub. Now, having seen *Psycho*, she won't take a shower, and she's getting very unpleasant to be around. What shall I do?"

———

$5.
> — Price tag still affixed to a geranium plant delivered to Joan Fontaine—a Christmas gift from David O. Selznick, who usually sent his stars lavish holiday presents . . . this a signal that Fontaine was in disfavor

Whatever You Say

LEAVE THEM WHILE YOU'RE LOOKING GOOD AND THANK GOD
FOR THE TRUST FUNDS MOMMA SET UP.
  — *Constance Talmadge*'s reported wire urging sister Norma to
    join her in movie retirement as the silent-screen star expe-
    rienced difficulty making the transition to talkies

———

What is this, a memory test?
  — *Elizabeth Taylor*'s supposed response when a justice of the
    peace asked the names of her previous husbands before
    officiating at yet another of her marriages

———

Miss Garbo says to say she is not in.
  — *Gustaf Norin,* butler-chauffeur, dutifully and literally car-
    rying out Greta Garbo's order when she was in a particu-
    larly remote mood, "I am not at home to anyone—
    remember, *not anyone!*"
*When she hired Norin, according to biographer Frederick Sands,
Garbo's first instruction had been, "You must never let anyone into
the house unless I tell you to"—while handing him a gun.*

———

No, Norman's not here. But I'll be happy to stab you.
  — Manager of a Bates Motel in Nevada, responding to
    Psycho cultists who ask for Anthony Perkins's character

Quotable Hollywood

Why didn't you pay the bloody ransom?
— *Richard Harris* to his wife, when she greeted him at the door upon his return to their London home—after he'd gone out for a newspaper and a drink one night and disappeared for five weeks

Daddy, buy me that!
— *Marlene Dietrich*, whispering in the ear of director Tay Garnett upon spotting young newcomer John Wayne in a studio commissary—after she "looked him up and down as though he were a prime rib at Chasen's," Garnett once recalled

Mr. President, you've got your show to run and I've got mine.
— *Elvis Presley* to Richard Nixon in the Oval Office one morning in 1970, when the President noted the visiting entertainer's velvet outfit (including cape) and said, "Boy, you sure do dress kind of wild, don't you?"

Who *made* the picture, the shark?
— Furious friend of "Steve" Spielberg as they watched with disbelief when the 27-year-old wunderkind was not nominated for a Best Director Oscar while his *Jaws* was put up as 1975's Best Picture

Whatever You Say

Like hell you did!
— *Katharine Hepburn*'s response to a fan who, when refused
   an autograph, lashed out at the actress during the height
   of her career: "How dare you refuse? We made you!"

What else could I do? I couldn't say anything—it would have
spoiled my party.
— *Norma Shearer,* explaining why she hadn't informed guests
   that neighbor Douglas Fairbanks, the evening's scheduled
   guest of honor before canceling because of illness, had
   died next door shortly after the diners sat down to eat—
   and partied until early morning, five hours after Shearer
   had learned of her friend's passing

It's our fault. We should have given him better parts.
— *Jack Warner*'s reaction to Ronald Reagan being elected
   governor of California

And, believe me, *Bedtime for Bonzo* made more sense than what
they were doing in Washington.
— *Ronald Reagan,* commenting on the Capital scene prior to
   his presidency, comparing it to his 1951 film

No.
>   — *Henry Fonda,* when asked in a *Playboy* interview if he'd
>   thought much of Ronald Reagan's ability as an actor

———•———

Survival.
>   — *Lauren Hutton,* when asked her greatest achievement

———•———

None.
>   — *Brigitte Bardot,* at 60, when *Vanity Fair* asked her to name
>   the living person she most admired

*And when the magazine asked what one thing she'd change about
herself if she could, Bardot answered: "Nothing about me.
Everything about others."*

———•———

Everything.
>   — *Mae West,* revealing what she wanted to be remem-
>   bered for

Critic-isms

Critic-isms

Critics put you on a pedestal—and can't wait to tear you down.
— *Lauren Bacall*

I'm convinced they are descendants of Attila the Hun, Hitler, and Charles Manson.
— *Frank Sinatra* on critics

Actors should never read them. If you don't believe the bad ones, why should you pay attention to the good ones?
— *John Barrymore* on reviews

Every actor in his heart believes everything bad that's printed about him.
— *Orson Welles*

———

I can't remember ever staying for the end of a movie in which the actors wore togas.
— *Jimmy Cannon,* columnist

———

A FEW WELL-CHOSEN WORDS ABOUT BEN-HUR: Ho hum.
— *Esquire* review headline

———

And to Hell it can go!
— *Ed Naha,* reviewing *From Hell It Came,* a 1957 horror flick

———

How can two people who look so good act so bad?
— *Gene Shalit,* on NBC's *Today* show, reviewing Ali MacGraw and Dean-Paul Martin in 1979's *Players*

———

Sharon Stone has made a fortune from her movies, so who says you can't get something for nothing?
— *Jeff Giles,* writing in *Newsweek*

Critic-isms

Since making her debut . . . Ms. Candice Bergen has displayed the same emotional range and dramatic intensity as her father's dummy, Charlie McCarthy.
  — *Harry and Michael Medved,* critics

What you said hurt me very much. I cried all the way to the bank.
  — *Liberace,* responding to a critic who panned a 1954 concert in New York

Critics are jealous. Like eunuchs, they can watch but cannot perform.
  — *Otto Preminger*

Extra! Extra!

Extra! Extra!

———•———

The main industry of Hollywood has never been the making of films, or even television. It is gossip.
  — *Sheilah Graham,* a Hollywood columnist who thrived on it

———•———

Tell him everything, dahling, only don't make me dull.
  — *Tallulah Bankhead* to a worried friend about to be interviewed about the actress

———•———

You go through my garbage and hide in my plants. It's not what grownups should do for a living.
  — *Cher,* chiding tabloid "reporters"

Clint Eastwood was flirting with me, and I got very flustered. I was blushing because he treated me . . . as a woman. He took all the authority away from me.
— *Barbara Walters*

———

Most [interviewers] ask dour questions.
— *Paul Newman,* explaining why he often comes across as dour in stories written about him

———

No. Boring.
— *Henry Fonda,* when asked if he found interviews exhausting

———

I'd rather ride down the street on a camel than give what is sometimes called an in-depth interview. I'd rather ride down the street on a camel nude. In a snowstorm. Backward.
— *Warren Beatty*

———

This interview.
— *Groucho Marx,* when an interviewer asked, "What annoys you most?"
And when the interviewer asked if he had any regrets, Marx replied, "The fact that I agreed to this interview."

Extra! Extra!

Hollywood loved them as the addict loves the pusher.
— *Life* magazine on Hedda Hopper and Louella Parsons

———

That's the house that fear built.
— *Hedda Hopper*, pointing to her Beverly Hills home

———

The freedom of the press works in such a way that there is not much freedom from it.
— *Princess Grace* (nee Kelly) of the Monaco Grimaldis

———

It isn't what they say about you—it's what they whisper about you.
— *Errol Flynn* on the Hollywood scene, which he gave
    plenty to whisper about

———

I'll never do the kind of book that people try to do on me . . .
    I'm not going to write anything about my deep personal life. I don't understand why people care about things like that.
    I mean I'm sure you've slept with one or two people, too, if that's your sport, and I certainly don't want to hear about it. So why would anyone be interested in whom I've been to bed with?
— *Katharine Hepburn*

I hope the next time she's crossing the street, four blind guys come along driving cars.
— *Frank Sinatra* on biographer Kitty Kelley

—·—

Oh, sure, every one. Where there's smoke, there's fire. Make up some more if you want to. They're all true. Booze, broads—all true.
— *Robert Mitchum,* when asked by critic Roger Ebert, "Are all the rumors about you true?"

—·—

Everything but what you print about me.
— *Lana Turner* to Hedda Hopper's "What's going on in your life?"

—·—

I improve on misquotation.
— *Cary Grant*

—·—

Goodbye, and don't betray me too much.
— *Simone Signoret* at the conclusion of an interview

If They Only Knew

If They Only Knew

Who the hell wants to hear actors talk?
— *Harry Warner*, who with three of his brothers founded the
studio that would pioneer sound pictures with 1927's *The
Jazz Singer*

We do not want now, and we shall never want, the human voice
with our films.
— *D. W. Griffith* in 1924, with talkies on the horizon

If I had known that, I would have put that eyepatch on 35 years
earlier.
— *John Wayne*, accepting his only Best Actor Oscar for his
role as an aging and ornery marshall in 1969's *True Grit*—
"a mean old bastard, a one-eyed, whisky-soaked, sloppy
old son of a bitch—just like me!" Wayne would say.

Talkies are spoiling the oldest art in the world—the art of pantomime. They are ruining the great beauty of silence. They are defeating the meaning of the screen.

— *Charlie Chaplin* in 1929

"Motion pictures need dialogue as much as Beethoven symphonies need lyrics," Chaplin protested while steadfastly refusing to speak in films until finally surrendering in 1940's The Great Dictator.

Every woman is afraid of a mouse.

— *Louis B. Mayer,* suggesting why young Mickey Mouse would never become popular

---

I just love everything about getting married.

— *Elizabeth Taylor* on May 6, 1950, when she married Nicky Hilton, husband No. 1

Who is this Sean Connery?

— *Ursula Andress* on the actor signed on as James Bond in 1962's *Doctor No*—she had to be persuaded to star opposite him.

If They Only Knew

Can't act. Can't sing. Slightly bald. Can dance a little.
— Studio talent evaluator's assessment after Fred Astaire's
first screen test in 1933, according to Hollywood legend

Too ugly to be a leading man, and not ugly enough to be a villain.
— *John Ford*'s assessment of a young Broadway actor named
Spencer Tracy—but signed him for his first major film
role anyway

Ye Gods, that horse face!
— RKO executive, his identity lost to posterity, reacting to
the screen test of young Katharine Hepburn, fresh off
Broadway in the early Thirties

Why did you throw away $500 on that big ape? Didn't you see
his ears when you talked to him? And those big feet and hands?
Not to mention that ugly face.
— *Jack Warner* to the minion who signed Clark Gable

I wouldn't pay $50,000 for any damn book, any time.
— *Jack Warner*, refusing to purchase movie rights to *Gone
with the Wind*

Into the Sunset

Into the Sunset

———— • ————

Getting old ain't for sissies.
   — *Bette Davis* in later life

———— • ————

A man is not old until regrets take the place of dreams.
   — *John Barrymore*

———— • ————

I'm getting old. I've got two more years, at least, then I'll have to go in for the face-lift.
   — *Cher,* planning ahead on her 26th birthday

———— • ————

I hear commercials for people over 50, and I think, "Oh my God, that's *me!*" I just hope they don't start giving me a discount at the movies.
   — *Cher,* a quarter-century later

Quotable Hollywood

Thirty-six is great when kids 12 to 17 still whistle.
— *Marilyn Monroe*, when asked about turning 36

From which direction?
— *Groucho Marx* to a woman who told him she was "approaching 40"

Sometimes they just sit there in stunned silence, amazed that I'm still alive and moving.
— *Marlene Dietrich*, while still drawing sellout audiences in her 70s

Oh, Jim, weren't we beautiful then?
— *Ava Gardner* to onetime co-star Stewart "Jim" Granger two weeks before her 1990 death at age 68

Considering the alternative, it feels wonderful.
— *Maurice Chevalier*, when asked on his birthday how it felt to be 70

The hell with it. I'm 72.
— *Frank Sinatra*, deciding to resume smoking

Into the Sunset

I'll be 80 this month. Age, if nothing else, entitles me to set the record straight before I dissolve. I've given my memoirs far more thought than any of my [six] marriages. You can't divorce a book.
— *Gloria Swanson*

————

The hardest years in life are those between 10 and 70.
— *Helen Hayes* at 83

————

If I'd known I was gonna live this long, I'd have taken better care of myself.
— *Jimmy Durante,* who lived into his mid-80s

————

I can't afford to die. I'm booked. I'd lose a fortune.
— *George Burns,* well into his 90s

————

Are you still around?
— *Adolph Zukor,* at age 99, to 74-year-old Jack Benny when they crossed paths in a country club dining room

Quotable Hollywood

People keep asking me how it feels to be 95, and I tell them I feel just as good as I did when I was 94.
— *George Burns*
Burns lived to 100, still professing: "You can't help getting older— but you don't have to get old."

You know what I want? I want yesterday.
— *Natalie Wood* to actress sister Lana not long before she drowned in 1981 at age 43

When my time comes, just skin me and put me right up there on Trigger, just as if nothing had ever changed.
— *Roy Rogers,* looking ahead to rejoining his loyal steed, who was stuffed and on display at the old Hollywood cowboy's museum in California

---

The only thing I worry about is dying without a cigarette in my mouth.
— *Bette Davis,* looking ahead on her 70th birthday

There are many ways to die in bed, but the best way is not alone.
— *George Burns*

Into the Sunset

Old Errol died laughing. Can you beat that?
— *Tony Britton*'s cable to fellow Brit actor Trevor Howard
on the 1959 demise of playboy pal Errol Flynn

———

Come now, Bela, quit putting us on.
— *Peter Lorre,* viewing the body of Hollywood's Count
Dracula at Bela Lugosi's 1956 funeral

———

I'll go without knuckling under.
— *W. C. Fields,* an agnostic, during his final illness in 1946
Yet he was caught reading the Bible in a hospital bed and explained,
"Just looking for loopholes."

About the Author

GEORGE SULLIVAN was a Boston reporter/columnist/editor and Boston University journalism professor whose stories have been featured in *The New York Times*, *Washington Post*, and *USA Today*, as well as in national magazines. This is his tenth book.

He and his wife, Elizabeth, reside in Belmont, Massachusetts—that's not far from Concord, the hometown of Ralph Waldo Emerson, who once sniffed, "I hate quotations."